Book 4
Deep Sea Danger

Reading Practice

her
serve
nerve
stern
over
finger
stinger

sir
girl
bird
first
stir
twirl
whirl

earn
search
pearl
heard
early

hurt
curl
turn
burn
lurch
disturb

word
world
worth
work
worm

At the bottom of each page of text, some multisyllable words are split up for the reader.

Contents

Chapter 1 The Sea   page 1

Chapter 2 Breakfast is Served!   page 4

Chapter 3 The Monster Under the Boat page 10

Chapter 4 Stingers!   page 13

Vocabulary:

drifted — gently carried along by water or air

twirled — turned round and round quickly

surface — the top of the water

whimper — cry with a soft, trembling voice

sternly — strictly

lurking — waiting threateningly where you cannot be seen

unfurl — unroll, unfold, spread out

hurl — to throw with great force

lurch — sudden staggering or leaning movement

twitch — to jerk or move suddenly and quickly

Chapter 1
The Sea

Zak and Mim slept in the boat. It drifted along the river and out to sea. Early, at first light, Mim stirred. "The sea!" she said to herself.

drift ed   ear ly   her self

"It's a good thing we fixed the boat," Mim thought, as she checked the hole in the boat. She did not want to disturb Zak. "I am so hungry," she whispered. "I'll get to work." Mim slipped into the water.

dis turb   whis pered

She searched for clams on the seabed. Seaweed curled and twirled around her. "This water world is so cool!" she said to herself.

sea bed   sea weed   wa ter

Chapter 2
Breakfast is Served!

Mim collected the clams and came up to the surface. "Breakfast is served!" she said. "Oh, it's so early!" Zak murmured and turned over to sleep.

coll ect ed   sur face   mur mured

"I'm an expert at this," Mim said, as she worked to open the clams. "Pass me the dagger," said Zak. "I want to learn how to do it."

ex pert   dagg er

Zak stuck the dagger in the clam and turned it. The dagger slipped.
"My finger! It hurts!" he whimpered as he sucked his finger.

dagg er   fin ger   whim pered

Mim looked at him sternly. "Look and learn," she said and took the clam. "Look, Zak, this isn't a clam! There's a little surprise in this one!"

stern ly   sur prise

"A pearl!" Zak cried. "This must be worth a lot! We can sell it! We could earn a lot of money!" "Or maybe we can trade it later," said Mim.

may be   la ter

Mim tucked the pearl safely in her pocket. "I'm glad I came on this journey," she said, as she dipped her legs in the water. "It has been worth it." Zak was in a world of his own. He hadn't heard a word she'd said.

safe ly   pock et   jour ney

Chapter 3
The Monster Under the Boat

Suddenly, Zak heard Mim cry out. "My leg, I've been stung! It hurts so much!" Zak leaned over to see. "It feels like a burn!" she said, nursing her leg.

sudd en ly   nurs ing

Zak looked under the boat. He saw a massive jellyfish monster. Its long stingers were lurking under the boat. They curled and unfurled, waiting to attack.

sting ers   lurk ing   un furled

"Stay in the boat!" Zak yelled and hurled himself into the sea. As he jumped, the boat lurched and tipped over. "No!" Mim cried, as she fell in the water after him.

wa ter   af ter

Chapter 4
Stingers!

The long stingers began working their way around Zak and Mim. Like giant worms, they curled around them, twitching, twirling.

gi ant   twitch ing   twirl ing

Zak held the talisman in his fist. Then he turned into a big turtle. The worm-like stingers curled around the turtle. They stung him again and again, but he snapped at the stingers with his beak.

tur tle   sting ers

Snap! Snap! One by one, the stingers fell down to the seabed below.

Mim looked on as the turtle ripped the monster to shreds. The turtle swam up to the surface.

sea bed   mon ster   sur face

Later on, Mim sat on the turtle's back. They surfed on the waves. Mim held on to the turtle's shell with one hand. In the other, she held the pearl.

la ter   tur tle   oth er